Color Me Human

By
The Hermit

Table of Contents

Dedication

Dedicated to Evelyn D. Mansfield. "You always knew that I could do this. Rest in peace, Mom."

Acknowledgment

First, I have to thank my sister, Melinda Jones, whose unwavering support has helped so much in making this possible. Also, my dear friend and biggest fan, Dixie M'Lynn, without whom the final chapter of this book would not have been possible. And to all my family and friends, on and off social media, who believed in me even when I didn't. I thank you all.

About the Author

I was first introduced to the hermit (Keith Mansfield) via a collaboration he had done with a mutual writer friend. I went to his Facebook page and began reading his own work. I was moved by his poetry. Keith's work is equally profound and prolific, moving, incredibly inspiring and beautiful. I have faith that the works contained in this volume will touch a chord somewhere deep within you. I know that his words have done that for me.

Dixie M'Lynn

One day, while doing nothing in particular, I heard my late mother's voice in my head just as clear as day. She told me the same thing she had often said to me throughout my life: "Keith, I know you can write." So I found an old notebook and pencil, sat down, and penned this poem. It was the first sober poem that I had ever written.

Chapter One

We are the Lost

I am one of the Lost,
Broke and defeated,
My soul bears the cost,
Of a history repeated.

Bankrupt of desire,
And with plundered esteem,
I failed to aspire,
Too broken to dream.

None will know,
The lies we exhaust,
We reap what we sow,
We are the lost.

The Renaissance

I came out of
The land of lost souls.
Rum-soaked and staggered,
Looking for my bottle
Amidst the scattered chaos
Of broken dreams.

When, on my last day,
In a moment born from electric nightmares
And stinging honesty,
Came clarity.

A moment unequaled.

Reborn in a renaissance
Of mind and spirit,
I am but a child.

You Couldn't Know

How can I tell you about me now,
When you knew nothing of before?

Before, when I walked through fire,
Just to feel it burn;
To feel nothing in oblivion.

When dying seemed like the next best thing,
And tomorrow was best Left to optimists,
While yesterday hung like a noose.

So I burned it all down!

Here But Not Here

Here but not here,
I'm seen, but not;
My cries go unheard,
Alone and forgot.

Huddled in shadows
Were no sane dwell,
My existence shrouded
By obsessions spell

Too broken to crawl,
And too weary to shout,
There's no end to it all,
No avenue out.

But on my visionless eyes
Fell a new day's light,
And with the golden sunrise
Came a new will to fight.

Lean On Me

Lean on me,
I will be your crutch
When life breaks you.

Talk to me,
So my ears
Can hear your pain.

My back is strong,
So share with me your burden.

Call me your friend,
And we will walk together.

My Search for Peace

And, in my quest to find peace,
I searched the four corners
Of the land.

I searched the wooded cabins,
Of the high peaks;
The white sand beaches,
And the shifting desert sands;

But no peace could be found.

"Maybe, only heaven holds
The peace that I seek?"

At that moment, I heard a voice,
As soft and sweet as a mother's touch:

"Why do you search for that
Which you have yet to create for yourself?"

So I went home,
And apologized to those around me
For my absence.

The coffee tasted somehow better
That I had remembered.

Compassion Speaks

Compassion speaks
With gentle hands,
Drying the tears
That torment commands.

Compassion speaks
From hearts that care,
Breaking the chains
Of binding despair.

Compassion speaks
To the face of hate:
"May the spirit of mercy
Guide your fate."

Arrogance

In my arrogance,
I thought I knew better;
That I was somehow wiser,
Than the demons
That plagued me.

But arrogance affords me.
No wisdom.

And clarity must be won by trial.

Please Tell Me

Please tell me
How true love feels.

Can you see it in her gaze?
Will her eyes tell a tale,
That a thousand words could not?

Can you hear it?
In the soft whispers
That she saves only for you?

Can you taste it on her lips;
Or smell it in passing?

Do your senses reel
When she dances in your memory?

Please tell me!

Reflections

The time has come,
When all of my yesterdays,
Have invaded my todays.

A morbid reflection;
A history of broken dreams,
And the wreckage in human souls
Left in the wake
Of an ego's rage.

When the musings
Of my tomorrow's never,
Becomes today's gospel,
The hole looms deep.

Would You Cry

Would you cry?
If sold away,
And struggled to live,
For just one more day?

Would you cry?
At the whips crack,
And wince in pain,
With a bloodied back?

Would you cry?
All alone at night,
In your silent torment,
Too broken to fight?

Would you cry?
When in heaven's light,
You're risen on high,
To end your plight?

Would you?

I Will Be There

When black is white
And the day is night,
And your world becomes shrouded
By a veil of fright,
I will be there.

When your best-laid plans
Crumble to dust,
And the pain of defeat
Like a knife has been thrust,
I will be there.

When Lost is all hope,
Washed away with the rain,
And no Light can be seen
Through the endless pain,
I will be there.

When you need a hand
To dry your tears,
And keep you safe
From the tormenting fears,
I will be there.

The Torment of the Innocent

Sobs,
Thunder claps forewarning
A father's fury,
Usher in tears of pain
From a child's soul

"What have I done, Daddy?"
Silent questions
Tormenting the fragile minds
Of the innocent.

A tiny mind,
Devoid of thought;
A tiny body,
Incapable of motion,
Caught in the grips
Of paralyzing fear.

Broken is the trust
In light of the leather,
Threatening the peace
Of a child's world.

In the wake of the pain,
And a world's broken skies,
One question remains,
"Why, Daddy, Why?"

I Shall Write Myself Wings

Leave me here,
Among the broken pieces
Of a fractured world;
For it is through imagination
That I find a kinder world;
And with ink and quill,
I shall write myself wings,
To fly above the fray.

The Bright Lights of Eden

Stepping from the bright lights of Eden,
And into the shadows
In this new world,
I found misery, pain,
And the disenchanted masses;
Wandering through their lives,
Grasping for any life-line,
To appease their security.
I turned,
To make my way back
To the beauty I had once known,
Only to find it
The door had been walled over
By mistrust and discontent.

Where had my Eden gone?

Real Men Don't Cry

Suck it up, buttercup!

Where's your skirt!

Walk it off,
Real men don't cry!

Pain,
Like a caged lion,
Rages against its capture;
Coming out sideways,
Oozing through cracks in the spirit.

Coward!
Real men don't cry!

They told me that you didn't make it.
And in the blink of an eye,
You were gone.

I cried.

I See You

I see your face in pink,
Newborn unto the world.

I see your face
In shades of red,
Your flame
Dancing hard against the night.

I see your face in ghostly white,
The frozen winds of fear
Biting at your very soul.

In all your colors,
I see you.

I Was Once Your Child

I was once your child;
Born of your blood,
And raised in the rubble
Of your broken dreams.
I wander now,
In places where mercy
Dares not tread;
For in this hell,
There are no angels;
Only the faces of the forgotten,
The lonely and the broken.

Born of your blood;
I was once your child.

A Hermit's Life

Darkness is the absence of light,
Of hope.

Lived in the shadows is this Hermit's life;
For the light is a harsh critic,
Always seeming to shine just out of reach;
Seen only as shards and slivers.

From the corners of crowded rooms
I watch the dance,
But I can't seem to figure out the moves;

Stumbling over my own presence,
I've made peace with the darkness.

Life is simpler here.

Now, at fifty-nine years old, I find myself tired, living in a body tortured by my hand. The wilt and resolve to keep going dwindle with every passing day, so I write. My notebook, a trusted friend, and my pencil are my weapons of choice.

The Sounds of Silence

Have you ever heard?
The sound silence makes
When there's nothing left to say?

Once, I heard the silence
In a pair of glaring eyes,
Deafening in their anger;

And once again
In her footsteps
As she turned to walk away.

Sometimes

Sometimes,
I fall into dreams of belonging,
Only to wake up
Beside myself;
Lost in the division
Between light and dark;
Between what was,
And what is?

Sometimes,
I find myself
Shuffling through the ashes
Of my burnt bridges,
Kicking
At the shards of burnt memories
Just to see how much has survived.

Chapter Two

The Terrace of Jones

The Terrace of Jones,
Where lies buried the bones,
Of a childhood spent wild and free;
Where balance on the rails,
Were life's wins and life's fails?
My sisters, my best friends and me.

We grew, and we learned,
We longed, and we yearned,
For the world beyond its dead end;
Oh, to see all the sites,
The cities, the lights,
And the heights we knew we'd ascend.

Now, heavy fall the years,
With life's joy and life's tears,
And with age weighing heavy on our bones;
We can look back and smile,
Despite the long while,
On our days spent on The Terrace of Jones.

Where the Steel Rails Run

I close my eyes in dreams,
They carry me, once more,
To where the steel rails run.

I find you now,
Shrouded in your veil of green;
Overgrown with memories,
And like all
That stands in the face of time,
A sentinel of what was.

But I remember
Only what was your glory;
And of my days spent there.

Where once led a path
To adventures untold,
Now lays my path
To my memories of yesterday.

Our Lady Bloomfield

We came to know her,
A lady fair;
And she's still held close,
With reverent care.

Our cradle of youth,
Where our life would unroll,
With a peaceful grace,
She nurtured our soul.

She showed us the beauty,
Of the natural world,
Where our dreams would sprout,
And life was unfurled.

She taught us to cherish
Her small-town charm,
Whether living on Main Street,
Or the family farm.

We may wander far,
With life and career,
But our lady Bloomfield
We'll always hold dear.

New York Summers

If I listen,
I can still hear the crickets
Of New York summers,
Playing their songs.

How green lay the hills
Where the white-tails roam;
And the land was seen to smile
With a contented grace
That asphalt and concrete
Just can't muster.

Someday, I'll go home.

The Scents of Youth

The freshly cut grass,
And the Lilac flower;
The smell of Black Walnut,
And a pie to devour.

The freshly waxed hall,
Of the school in the fall;
The smell of glue,
And the cafeteria too.

The scents of our youth,
We have, and we hold;
It's our memory's truth,
In stories told.

#140

And there I sat,
Looking for peace
In the silence of nature;

But there were the birds,
Chirping, chirping, chirping;
But they sounded so pleased with their song.

And the crickets,
With their symphony of thousands;
Brought me back to the summers
Of my youth;

There was the flutter of leaves,
As the breeze broke through the trees,

And there I sat;
Being regaled by nature's concerto,
Right where peace had found me.

Sweet Child

Oh, sweet child;
May the day
Lay gentle
On your fragile wings,
And the night
Fall tender on your heart;
For tomorrow, you blossom,
And cast your beauty
Upon the world.

#248

Mother,
Please speak to me;
If only
A whisper in a dream.

Sing me a lullaby
Tender and sweet,

Tell me a story,

For there is still magic
In a mother's voice,
If only in my memory.

An Organized Lad

What fun is to be had,
With an organized lad?
His ducks, placed all neatly in rows.
With all the starch in his collar,
He's wound too tight to holler,
Even if they chopped off his toes!

But life is best seen,
From the spaces in between,
Where random is the nature and course.
Where life's moments, most treasured,
Come neither marked nor measured,
By any hint of regret or remorse.

Such Moving Wonders

I want to live in my art;
Build a house,
That floats on a stream of words;
Nights of moonlit wonder,
And days,
Of sun-filled possibilities.

Discovering the lost days,
Of sad songs and fairytales.

A crumbling world,
Reclaimed,
By the mystical denseness of a moment.

The imagination holds such moving wonders.

Be a Butterfly

There I am,
Stuck in my cocoon
Of fear and hate;
Seemingly safe in my emptiness.

I choose to break
From the confines
Of my cocoon;
To join the world,
Morphed,
Ready to spread my wings
And bring a new beauty
To the world.

I choose to be a butterfly.

Painting Today

I sat in the early morning,
And painted today,
A landscape of blue and gold.

I painted the wonders of life,
In shades of green,

And I painted my peace,
On the clouds, in white.

A more glorious picture,
Has yet to be laid before me.

Ode to Mothers

Live softy in your grace,
And mark your peace
With humble offerings.

Speak gently your wisdom,
For it is a needed gift.

Bear your heart,
And whisper your love
To our infant ears.

Place your healing hand,
Upon my cheek,
And renew my spirit.

Move now,
To where your comfort lay,
And live softly in your grace;
Your work for today is done.

Becoming

No longer a slave to this world,
I become part of it;

My imagination soars
When I unbind myself from the concrete.

Soaring on waves of thought,
I become the bird's song;
My melodies,
Carried on the breeze.

I become the dirt
Between my toes,
And the smell of wildflowers
That graces my nose;

I am free.

It Is Here

It is here,
Where my thoughts turn to magic,
And dreams,
Dance in the moonlight,

Here, in this place,
Where peace flows,
Like rivers through my mind,
That I shall build my house of words.

I search my mind's junk drawer,
Looking for words that are classic and time-held.
Words that I've set aside for the perfect moment;
Words now lost among all the other bits and pieces,
All the odd fragments that time has marooned there.
All just waiting for their chance to shine.

Ahh, maybe tomorrow.

Chapter Three

For Ava

Risen from the cradle
On heavenly wings,
Listen now for the song
As your destiny sings.

May you weather life's storms
With amazing grace,
For in you lies a warrior
With an angel's face

Here and Gone

Here and gone
Are all things.

Time shall never
Hold the hours,
That I may linger in a moment.

For just as surely
As the dawn will break
On a new tomorrow,

On all of my days,
The sun will surely set;

And the hours, well-lived,
Shall be the gold that fills my coffers.

Between Yesterday and Nowhere

The cold air sharpens my breath,

And my rhythm,
So fluent in dreams is lost
To consciousness.

Stumbling on cracks in the sidewalk,
I lose my place,
Only to start again where I find myself;

Halfway between yesterday,
And nowhere.

The Memory of a Moment

When the mysterious heavens
Blossom with the light
Of a billion stars,
Hold me in their glory,
To savor the while,
So that, in their fading,
I shall be left
With the memory of a moment.

Exhale the Day

I breathe in the hours,
And exhale the day. Holding,
In this moment of reflection,
As images pass,
In a slide show
Of softer memories
Playing against the darkness
Of tired eyes.

Sinking deeper,
I drift away.

Sit With Me

Come, sit with me
In the quiet hours,

Share with me
Moments, unspoken;

Let the silence
Foster our peace,
And gently ease our spirits.

Tomorrow can wait.

Before Time

Before time,
There was simply day and night,
Light and darkness;

The change of seasons
Marked our wanderings.

Existence marked our purpose.

Our steps had meaning;
Our breath gave life to the wind.

But all that was before,
Before time,
Before the tic-tock of the clock.

Life has become so simple,
Hasn't it.

Wonderous

Oh,
To weed out,
The large and unwieldy parts;

To live
For the smallest of thoughts,
To move with grace
On a pauper's fare;

To exist for a moment
In small wonders;

Such peace.

#134

Don't look for me
In your paint-by-numbers world,
I am not there;
I exist outside
Your stifling convention.
My own picture I create,
My own space,
My own lines to color within.

I am the scribbling child;
With a defiant grin.

Catch me if you can!

Once bound by convention,
I've jumped the garden wall
And found a new path.

#138

I dislike winter.

Winter reeks of death;
All that survives
Must be stubborn and prickly,
Like the evergreens.

I can be stubborn and prickly,
Waiting for the pastels of spring
To soften my edges;
To create some,
A warmer version of myself.

Though,
I can still be stubborn and prickly.
Some edges never soften.

Wandering Out

With every breath,
I sink deeper;
Wandering out
From my center,

Far afoot;
And the light of heart.

Now, all places,
Within my reach, fall.

I Still See You

Sometimes
I still see you,
There, in that place
Where hope still lingers.

Other times,
You come in dreams,
Only to fade with the coming dawn.

But somehow, always remaining,
Just out of reach.

A Foreigner in a Foreign Land

I come from the agony of life;
From the pain,
To this place of mercy.

Here, where kindness
Is met with kindness,
I am caught, suspicious;
A foreigner in a foreign land,
With no coin to pay the piper.

I called past yesterday,
But tomorrow rings hollow;
And yet, I move forward.

For no longer
Do I pay rent for yesterday,
Only today.

#444

Dance with me,
Here, in the dark;
Hold my heart
For the length of a song,
And I shall ask
Nothing more.

Nobodies Home

I caught myself,
Staring into the empty space
Behind my eyes.

It held the color
Of a foggy winter's night;

The streetlights,
Casting their nebulous glow
On empty streets.

The lights are on, but there's nobody home,

Again!

Bound To Reality

She bowed her head
To the stars, in reverence,
And prayed,
That one of her many dreams,
Cast into the night,
May find its way home.
Though, all she could see
With her bowed head,
Was her feet in the dirt,
Bound to a realty
That she couldn't shake.

Dance of Souls

Gather all your souls,
And move, wide-eyed,
To the splendor
Of the cool forest green;
There to dance
Upon its needled mat,
Until the dying tight
Leaves us,
To dream of softer days.

How Far

How far is it,
To the outer edge of myself?
To that place
Where thought overtakes
My understanding,
And all that I have known,
Asks new questions.

I would love to know.

The Price of Admission

I am here,
But you can't see me.

I'm just another face in the crowd
That can't afford
The price of admission
To the big table;

So I make my peace beneath it.

I like your shoes.

A Future's Mosaic

I take from this world;
Bits and pieces,
A future's mosaic
Of scattered memories
And lessons learned.

A work of art
As yet, unfinished.

#411

Tell me not of tomorrow,
But as a surprise,
Let it be gifted;
For I shall be no better off
For the knowing.
Because,
In anticipation's absence,
The dream is lost,
And without dreams,
Tomorrow is lost.

Still, She Sang

I saw a bird,
Sitting on a wire
Trying with all her will
To hold firm
Against life's raging storm;

But still, she sang.

Pieces

There are pieces of me,
Pieces that I share,
Pieces that I hand out freely,
Like business cards
With embossed lettering
On fine stock.

The refined, rehearsed,
And well-polished pieces.

But there are pieces,
That I keep just for me.

The unfinished and unkept pieces;

The shattered glass,

The scattered puzzle pieces
That have yet to be fit

The pieces that may never fit.

Color me, Human

Color me red;
Branded a savage,
My trail of tears
Still looms long.

Color me black;
For the chains that
Still, bind me
To hate and ignorance,
Are not yet broken.

Color me yellow;
For misunderstanding
And fear,
Still, brand me the enemy.

Color me brown;
For the persecution of all,
For the bellicose rhetoric
Of the few,
Still marks me.

Color me human;
For my blood runs
Just as red,
And my tears fall
Just as wet,
In the wake of dehumanizing hate.

For Kiley

Wrap me gently
In your memory,
And carry me with you.
So that,
When the wind blows,
And the thunder
Scares you from your peace,

I will be with you.

Life's Shifting Sands

I have for you, compassion,
To soften your days,
And ease the bitterness,
Of the blackening haze.

I'll give you my shoulder,
A home for your tears,
And a loving touch,
To assuage your fears.

And accept from me, love,
To warm your heart,
And make gentle the hours,
That we spend apart.

All these I give,
With loving hands,
To keep your soul grounded,
In life's shifting sands.

Can You Hear Me

Can you hear me?
In that place beyond time,
Where mortals fear to tread?

Do your eyes still see me?
Drifting,
Upon this ocean, alone?

Do you cast my name to the wind?

Can you feel my heart?
Beating still, for you?

In Them, I Will Know

And in your weakest hour,
Your eyes will betray your heart,
For in them, I will know,
That I am your world.
That I am the thief
That steals your breath,
And strips away your fear;
The sun that warms your days,
And the stars
That brightens your darkest nights.
I will read in your eyes,
All the words
That fear,
Has robbed from your voice;
And in that moment,
Your soul will be laid bare.

The Spectator

I love to read poetry, especially the books of the masters. I am at peace in someone else's world. Alive but not living.

But I have lived! I've beaten my head against life's hard edges, never trusting in its softness. It always seemed like a ruse to lure me into something I couldn't see coming.

So now I play the spectator. Watching today's youth beat their heads against the same hard edges, reliving the pain as if it were a newfound memory.

I wished I had listened to my parents.

She was far too gentle for this world,
And the world,
Far too vicious and relentless
To ever bow to her grace;
So, it took her,
And laid her to rest in memory.
But in a memory pure and unsullied;
A place out of reach
Of the day's chaos.

Rest now, your gentle soul,
Your work is done.

He is of time,
The new and the old;
She is of nature,
The blue and the gold.

He is the line,
That threads through our days;
She is the fury,
And the sun's golden rays.

He is the hours,
Spent watching the stars;
She is our nature,
Our beauty, our scars.

He is the withering,
That comes in vain;
She's the dried leaves,
And blackberry stains.

She is of nature,
Her forces to command;
He is of time,
Our line in the sand.

Chapter Four

Arrogant Eyes

We see the world,
Through arrogant eyes,
But never do we listen
To her angry cries.

Concrete and metal,
Monuments in steel,
They change how we think,
And warped how we feel.

Postage stamp parks,
Mere freckles of green,
The last meager remnants,
That shows where we've been.

Listen to the whispers,
Of the wind through the trees,
And the cries of the Mother,
Singing her pleas.

Listen to the birds,
The rivers and streams,
And hear of their hope,
Be part of their dreams.

We see the world,
Through arrogant eyes,
But never do we listen,
To her angry cries.

My Peace Has Teeth

The wolves,
They howl at my door;
On my perceived loneliness
They wish to pray,
But my peace has teeth;
Defending a voice,
And giving no ground.

Fresh Eyes

I need to see the world,
From a different point of view,
Through fresh eyes.

Maybe,
I'll lie down on a city street,
Just to look up;

Or perhaps I'll parachute,
From ten thousand feet,
Just to see as the birds do;

Maybe I should dawn my sunglasses,
To shade my eyes
From the world's harsh glare.

Or maybe, just maybe,
I'll find a mirror
And look into my own eyes;

Where the real mystery lies.

The Human Raptors

The human raptors,
Perched high on their ivory towers;
Power-starved, hungry,
And feigning omnipotence,
They puff out their vested chests;
Endlessly searching
For Glory's next conquest.

When their endorphins surge
From drinking power's nectar;

They look to the weak,
To assuage their hunger.
Leaving none but the brave,
To defend their ranks.

But no more in victory,
Shall their lives be claimed.

I Want To Believe

I want to believe in Superheroes.

I want to see them
Flying the skies,
Their red capes,
Dancing in the wind;
Delivering to the world
Some long-forgotten wisdom,
Of a more noble purpose.

I want to believe
That their vision can pierce the chaos,
And bear witness to a greater truth.

I want to, once more,
See the world
With the wonder of a child's eye.

I want to believe in Superheroes.

My Truth

My truth,
That forbidden fruit;
Now runs
Down the chins
Of feral puppeteers;
Left to collect in puddles,
To be stomped underfoot
By the Armies of Delusion
Feigning their omnipotence.

But from the soles of their boots,
I shall gather
The seeds of my truth,
And, in the light
Of a new day,
To once more sow.

Ragamuffin

Ragamuffin child,
With a runny nose and dirty hands,
Building your new world
In a sandbox;

It's all so fresh.

Ragamuffin child,
With a runny nose and dirty hands,
Digging for your dinner
In the bombed-out rubble
Of home;

"Maybe something survived?"

Ragamuffin children,
I hope you find your tomorrow.

Wings of Peace

From an angry world,
I shall beg no mercy;

I will rise above it,
On the white wings of peace,
To a place,
Where hope paints my days;

And the warmth of love,
My nights.

Where Have All The Angels Gone

I saw a homeless man,
With his life in a backpack;
The dirt clinging to him
Like a cloak of bad memories.

I saw an old woman,
Eating her dinner from a cat food tin,
And watching her Wheel of Misfortune;
Reeking from the stench of loneliness,
And too feeble to bath.

I saw a child,
With a gaunt face and swollen belly,
And a piece of chalk,
Drawing her prince charming
On broken concrete.

I saw my reflection
In a pane of glass, I asked myself:

Where have all the angles gone?

#257

With temper ablaze,
You would
Burn down the world
Just to satisfy your pain;

Only
To piss on those burning,
And call it mercy!

Life's Waters

I swim through life's waters;
Looking to be refreshed,
To be somehow cleansed
Of the daily dirt and grime.

In an ocean of billions,
I find no solace;

I find the shallow depths are unsettling,

So, I search
For deeper waters to tread.

A Fire

Never shows the same face twice;
Nor will our leaders.

Their armies of delusion
Are Goose-stepping their way,
Backwards,
Into a dark tomorrow.

Oh, the sun will rise;
And summer will, once again,
Give way to fall,
As we carry the good fight,
From our righteous bunkers
Of well-manicured green;
Unleashing the pain
Of our passion's fury
Into the gritty, worn,
Grey concrete jungles
Of this land.

We will never surrender!

The Little Man

And there you are,
With your magnifying glass,
Burning your hate
Into the souls of the rare;
Your pain, for now,
Stands diverted.

And there you are,
Goading the strong
Into hollow victories,
While the meek, cower;
You laugh,
Your pain, for now,
Stands diverted.

And there you are,
Long in years,
And wallowing in your empty success;
You're not laughing;
Your pain, now,
Hangs from your soul
Like a tortured veil.

Enjoy the view.

He Walks Among Us

From his fiery realm,
We've raised the devil
To walk amongst our children.

He wears many faces,
But speaks with one voice.

Do you know him?
Have you seen his reflection?
Cast in the eyes of cowards
Disguised as men?

He calls out from our frailty,
A sermon of fear;

Can you hear him?
Because our children can.

I Want To See

I want to see hope;
But the darkness of a billion screams
Has veiled its face.

I want to know peace;
To taste its sweetness;
To drink it from a cup, overflowing,

Or has that vintage been marched under?

Can the veil be lifted?
Or have the seeds of these fruits
Been forever lost?

I want to know,
Because I wish to see a brighter tomorrow.

What Am I?

I am the anger,
Raging against the dark,
I am the hope,

The light, the spark;
I am the tears,
That wash away the sorrow,

I am the joy,
The light in tomorrow;
I am the pain,

The happy,
The sad;
I am the good,

The ugly,
The glad;
I am the silence,

That bump in the night,
I am the prayer
That brings the light;

I am all parts
That makes you whole,
I am your spirit,
I am your soul.

#150

I grow cold;
In the calloused hardness
Of a concrete world.

Softness,
Sharpened to razor's edge.

Words,
Like daggers,
Slice through fragile minds;
As hatred rubs salt
Into the open wounds.

Is this who we are?

I look in the mirror,
For answers.

The Godless Land

And,
Through the godless land,
I walked the path
Of martyrs and madmen;

Staring into broken windows
Where angels cower,
And the gluttonous mob
Devours the day.

How far we have come,
Only to walk backward
Into tomorrow.

Beggar's Church

I see you there,
Your shopping cart
Filled with old blankets,
Cardboard and yesterday's dreams;
Searching for a sympathetic doorway
To rest your cup;
And handing out blessings
To all that give tithes
To your beggar's church.

I see you there,

Clinging to your humanity
Like some abandoned puppy,
And praying that it, too,
Won't be lost.

Yes, I see you there.

Purity

What in this life
Do we deem as pure?

A newborn child,
Honey, Evil?

Even the winter's snows
Gather the breath of industry!

Maybe a fresh mountain spring
Before its waters are civilized;
Or a single note
Struck with timely perfection.

Silence is pure;
The night is pure.

Chapter Five

The Torchbearers

And then somewhere,
As days passed to years,
It was lost.
We had become the elder guard,
The keepers of tales old
And wisdom new.
No longer the hunters of Snipe,
Our youth, Long since Left behind
In those grassy fields and enchanted woods.
The future's endless possibilities
Have turned to numbered days,
Where victories
Are marked in sunrises,
And losses
In lonely sunsets.
Slowly, we fade
Into the dimming light of tomorrow,
Remembered only by those
Who choose to bear the torch?

Passing Time

I stumble through the morning,
Half dazed;

Going through all the motions
That somehow seem important.

I watch lips move on talking heads,
But I can't make out the words;

I'm a million miles away,

Trying to figure out
If I'm passing through time,
Or if I'm standing still
As time passes, me?

Dust Covered Memories

Dust covered memories
In layers of gray,

Barely recognizable now;

Recovered, one by one,
As if photos
From some long-forgotten cache.

Dimmed with age,
And edges tattered;

Some have faded,
Some are forever lost,
And some, still held dear.

Unburdened

Now,
As days pass
With an unencumbered swiftness,
I grow bold;
For regrets weigh heavy
On the frailty of age,
And I shall leave this world

Unburdened.

On The Occasion Of My61st Birthday

Slow the world
To the speed of an old man's gate;
For, I've fallen behind.

Hold still the passing day,
That I may rest in a moment.

Lend me your shoulder,
And a measure of grace;

Let me catch my breath,
Before you let me go.

#123

Of a life survived,
I sit today
In quiet reverence,
My coffee and memories, well-tended.

Slower now,
Days are passed
With humble pleasures:
Good music,
And an unhindered stroll.

Leaving tomorrow's struggles
Unattended,
I savor the wonder of now.

I find peace in days like these.

Ghosts of the Sonoran Desert

I can feel them;
The ghosts that haunt this place.
Their ancient dust
Turning swirls across the desert.

I hold out my hand,
Attempting to feel
Their dried, worn leather.

And on quiet nights,
When the air hangs still,
I can hear their voices
In the coyote's howl,
Telling me that I am home.

The Quiet

The quiet
Hangs no veil of loneliness
Over my soul;

I find my peace
In the silent hours,

Where my imagination
Wanders into the unknown,
I find wonder,

And within myself,
I take comfort.

The Best of You

(For Chelo)

I gaze upon your years;
To that place
Where true beauty lays,
To the heart of you,
To the soul of you.

Fear not
For what the thief of time
Has stolen,
For in his haste,
He has left the best of you.

Please Don't Leave Me There,

In that antiseptic wasteland.

We left mom there, scared and alone;
Where her fractured memories,
Were like a trunk of torn pictures
That she could no longer piece together;

Scared and alone, stripped
Of all things familiar.
Our lives had become more important than hers,
More important than our kindness.

And, if one day, your lives become
More important than mine,
Please don't leave me there.
Leave me on the side of the road,
Or at a highway rest stop,
I'll find my own way.

Dying is easy.

Self

I feel myself
Fading into what was,
Disappearing from the now
And into a campfire story
From yesterday.

You are the future,
And I am the past;

What will be.
Is yours to mold.
What was,
Is mine to tell.

Make Merry

Together,
Let us dance and sing
The song of ages;

We will make merry
While the sun still rests
Above the horizon;

And when the sun
Has lost its battle with the night,

We will dance in the moonlight,
Until,
Once more,
The sun casts our shadows
Upon the Earth.

Rest in Memory

She was far too gentle,
For this world;
And the world,
Far too vicious and relentless
To ever bow to her grace.

So it took her,
And laid her to rest in memory.

But it's a memory
Pure and unsullied;
A place where all the chaos
No longer reaches.

Judge Me Not

Judge me not
For my hobbled gate,
Crippled was I
In my fall from grace.

Judge me not
For my etched face,
It was bore
From weathering ridicule's storm.

Judge me not
For my toothless maw,
Lost were they
Gnawing free vice's chains.

Judge me not
For my twisted path,
For it brought me
Into the light of wisdom.

Water-Colored Nostalgia

Time,
Marked in water-colored nostalgia,
Paints my yesterdays
In subtle hues of fantasy.
A cottage in memory,
Carefully tended and displayed,
Beside an unfinished tomorrow.

Simple Days

Dreams retreat with the fog,
As the day breaks once more.

Rusty joints ache,
As they break free
From the idle night;

Coffee and music
Lubricate the dawn;
Pencils and poetry
Give it meaning.

I have found my peace,
In the gentle splendor
Of these simple days.

Life's Song

I hear life's song;
A melodic masterpiece
That lays gentle on my soul.

The thrashing tones of youth
Now, flow with a peaceful rhythm.

This, by far,
Has been my favorite part if the show.

A Portrait

It's not a bowl of fruit,
But it's still life.

They all have eyes,
But can they see?

Do they know that I'm here,
A world apart?

For the longest time, I stared;
Maybe I'd catch them flinching,
But all I caught was myself,
Standing there with my face hanging open.

Still, I'd like to believe
That there's life;
That they can see.

Call me crazy.

The Greatest Torment

I once saw a bee
That was too feeble to fly.
It just walked in circles,
With no place to go.

And I wondered:

Would that be me someday?
Too feeble to fly,
Wandering in circles with nowhere to go,
But still intent on getting there?

I pray for mercy,
For I can think of no greater torment.

Few are the days now,
When life's melody
Plays out in somber tones.

Nor do trumpets
Hail the conquering hero.

Each note,
Now, a masterpiece of wisdom and patience,
Is played to the rhythm
Of these gentler days.

Virgin Eyes

What,
In those virgin eyes
Do I behold,
But a new world's wonder;
And the joy in a moment.
Certainly not
The weight of knowing
Left imprinted on mine
By the crush of years.

Is it possible,
Can one ever recapture
The wonder found there,

In those virgin eyes?

I often wonder.

The Call of Years

Let us play,
And wring today's joy
From the morning dew;
For today,
The call of years falls silent
On my aging ears,
And tomorrow comes too soon.

I Am

In your mind,
I exist as a portrait
Painted by the hand of fate.
But I am more than what resides
Within that framed stillness.
I am the vibrance
Of the morning sun,
Painted in gold;
And the darkness
That haunts the night.
I am the good, the bad,
The happy, the sad.
I am a portrait of one,
Hung in a gallery of billions.
I am.

My Generation

I saw my reflection in a window,
It was the face of a generation.

We were the free birds,
The Cocaine generation;
Searching,
For Green Grass and High Tides,
But finding only
The Dark Side of the Moon.

And now we stand,
Gazing upon A Stairway to Heaven,
Unwilling, as yet,
To take the first step.

THE OLD OAK

In the days of your youth,
But a sapling were you;

Vibrant in color and vigor,
Standing strong
Against the passing storms;
Your roots holding fast;
Declaring this spot,
This place on Earth, yours.

You flourished;
Setting the seeds
Of a new youth to the winds.

Now, standing aged,
The vibrance of youth
Long since drained from your limbs,
You still hold purpose.

For you bear witness to what was;
Setting the young
On a course of wonder,
And boldly stating:

Learn from my scars and broken limbs,
The lessons of life.
For I was, too, but a young sapling.

The Grand Illusion

How far I have wandered
From the green days of youth.

Kool-Aid and Converses,
Lost,
To the grand illusion
That is maturity.

I think I'll go catch frogs.

A Moment with Grandpa

She gazed into his eyes,
With a child's wonder.
Her tiny fingers
Tracing out the lines on his face,
And she asked:
Grandpa, what's it like to grow old?
It's like a picture album,
Filled with old memories,
And a stiff old binding
That creeks when you open it.
Then she asked:
Grandpa, what's it like to die?

Peace, I hope.

The Mending

Move me
From the gathering storm,
And mend
My fraying edges;

Mellow me,
To the softness
Of early morning dew;

And with a whisper,
Lay me to rest,
On this sweetest of nights,
To dream of gentler days.

Leather-Bound and Embossed

I know this place.
I've seen it in the poems,
Of Shakespeare and Frost;
A world of wonder,
Leather-bound and embossed.

Oh, to build a house
Between its worn, dusty pages
And live in the rhythm,
Of the old bards and sages.

What a grand place, indeed;
To, between its dusty pages,
And in the shadows of its covers,
Leather-bound and embossed,
Be lost.

#231 (sonnet #2)

Show me where the water lilies rest;
Upon a pond of shimmering gold,
And let this scene of peace attest
To the beauty my eyes behold.

Shock to life, my senses dulled;
That they may revel in the hours,
And from the dreary shall I be annulled
To slumber beneath the bowers.

Oh, for an eternity in this place;
Here, where time stands still,
No more to run humanity's race
No more my coffers to fill.

And from this dream, should I never awake,
I pray the Lord my soul to take.

I saw a lizard with only one back leg, moving slowly and with no particular sense of urgency, through the shade of the spider plants on the back patio. I started to feel a sense of kinship in the amended purpose that age and survival had afforded us both.

Every morning, with the sunrise, we reinvent our purpose and renew our mark.

My mark will be left on those who choose to remember me. As for the lizard, his mark is left on me. Every day, defying natural selection, defying the odds, surviving.

I learned a lesson from that lizard.

Life sometimes throws a wrench into our well-ordered plans, and sometimes, we have to reinvent our purpose and find a new path to the shade.

Sometimes, we have to defy the odds.

The Fall

There's a numbness that comes
With the summer's fading color.
A resignation of comfort
To the cold dying.

Not everything survives
To be reborn.
Some things,
Are forever lost to the bitterness.

But when, once more,
We invest ourselves
In the vivid shades of rebirth,
When we push back
Against the dying,

Will we deem what's been lost
As necessary?

WITH A LITTLE HELP FROM A FRIEND

COMPILATIONS WITH: Dixie M'Lynn

Chapter Six

I saw you there,
With your tangerine hair,
And your lips of coral pink;
I couldn't help but stare,
At your crimson flare,
And the way you'd glance and wink.

I saw you, too,
Eyes brown, not blue,
In that T-shirt, aubergine.
Carnelian Chucks,
I thought, "Aw shucks;"
In the midday sun, citrine.

Oh my! Oh dear!
As you came near.
You asked, "What are you up to today?"
"Just sitting here,
Craving root beer,
Until you strolled my way."

So, off to the stand,
We walked, hand in hand,
For a dog and a root beer float;
And for one afternoon,
On a day in late June,
New love didn't seem so remote.

Glory Days

Glory days, a faded haze,
Of beer-soaked memories,
Held captive by my sins,
In a prison of my own device.

But I've pulled my sentence
From fate's bloody grasp.
My penance, I've shed in tears
That flood my soul.

I'll not beget more bitter regret,
Than what I've lost in you.

Wonder

What fun is to be had,
With an organized lad,
With his ducks placed all neatly in rows?
With all the starch in his collar,
He's wound too tight to holler,
Even if they chopped off his toes.

But life is best seen,
From the spaces in between,
When the spaces are filled by a friend.

My sweet friend, there is joy,
For such a starched boy,
If you teem with a saucy Ol' lass!
The birds and the bees,
On a soft sunset breeze,
Strolling barefoot through the grass.

So, come take my hand!
Let's depart this dry Land,
For a world where wonder won't end.

Partner

Move me to laughter,
Move me to tears,
Move to let go,
Of all my pent-up fears.

Hold me through madness,
Hold me through joy,
Hold me in memories,
Time won't destroy.

And I'll be your jester,
I'll recurve your frown.
Those burdens you carry,
I'll help put them down.

For the days we walk together,
Are the days we walk the best,
And even in the quiet hours,
We'll know that we are blessed.

What the night doesn't hide,
In speaks in shadows,
Cast upon the dim,
In voiceless vision,
In whispers.

Mysteries revealed
In sloe heart of night
To the vigilant,
To the brave;
While the dreamers sleep.

Falling Feather

All the white doves have fallen,
Symbols of peace exist no more;
Their ghosts, in broken form,
Haunt the battlefield,
And charred school yards.
Feathers fall like casings,
Of automatic ammunition,
While politicians ban,
The Grapes of Wrath.

To all of you who made it this far,
I sincerely thank you. You are troopers.

You can find me daily (well, almost daily)
On Facebook @The Hermit, or Instagram
@the.hermitdiaries.

Thank you again for reading, and remember:
Tum off the news, and turn on the music!

www.ingramcontent.com/pod-product-compliance
Lightning Source LLC
Chambersburg PA
CBHW071759120626
46550CB00002B/845